Lichfield Cathedral

extraordinary past, inspirational present, glorious future

Herkenrode glass detail

Lichfield Cathedral
extraordinary past, inspirational present, glorious future

CONTENTS

ARCHES ✠ ARCADES

The medieval builders didn't know when to stop. One spire would have been splendid; two magnificent; but they went one better for the glory of God and erected three. Almost 800 years later, Lichfield Cathedral is still inspiring visitors – but it's also become something of a conservation liability.

It was the same inside the building. Once the masons had grasped how to erect a 'gothic' arch, they couldn't resist putting them everywhere. When there weren't any more spaces to enclose with arches, they built rows of arcades against blank walls. With astonishing exuberance, they created one of the great glories of early English architecture.

The first Cathedral was dedicated in December 700 by Bishop Hedda, and drew pilgrims to the bones of St Chad for 400 years. A new building was begun in 1085, and was developed by Bishop de Clinton in the 1140s to cater for the growing crowds of pilgrims. But, within a few decades, English masons had begun dismantling his Norman structure and making their own bold statement of elegant Gothic design.

By the time the Black Death brought work to a stop in 1349, Lichfield Cathedral looked much as it does today. Three spires, an array of arches and arcades, the great wooden doors, and – uniquely – a level floor throughout so that even the weak, the old and the lame could worship God without any impediment.

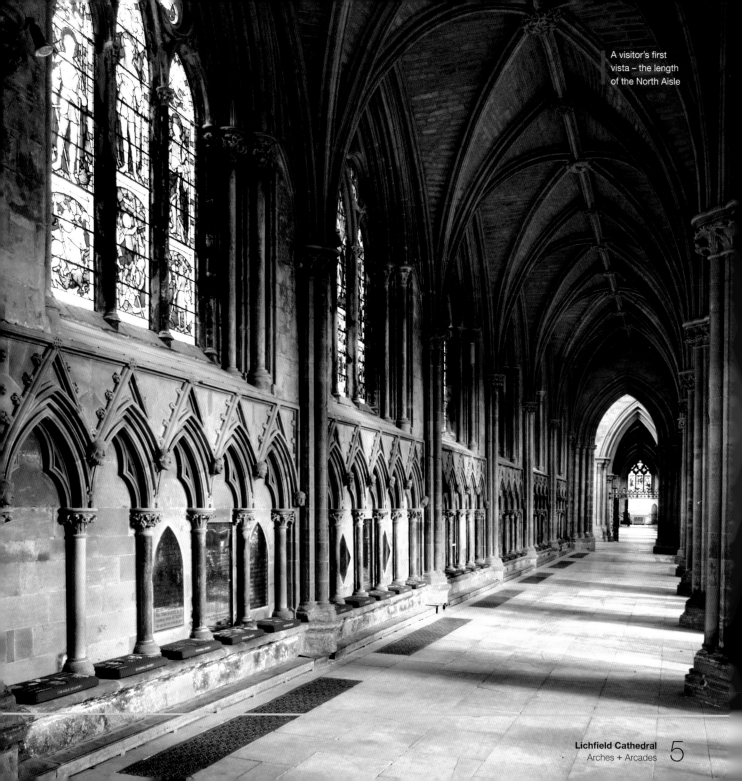

A visitor's first
vista – the length
of the North Aisle

The unforgettable view
of the Cathedral's
13th century Nave

Lichfield Cathedral
Arches + Arcades

An Epstein bust of Bishop Woods graces the intimate Pedilavium

The Cathedral organ, seen here from the Quire, has over 5000 pipes

WINDOWS ✠ SYMBOLS

Nobody is quite sure why the masons created Lichfield Cathedral just as they did, but they certainly meant to fill the building with a celebration of heavenly joy. For, inside, a riot of colour inspired drab lives, as surfaces were decorated with stories for people without learning.

Their beautiful wall paintings, however, were covered during the religious turmoil of the 16th century, and their coloured windows were smashed in the Civil War of the 17th century.

At the end of the 18th century, the French Revolution ended religious activity in Herkenrode – the richest women's abbey in the Low Countries. By 1801, its rare oil paintings and majolica floor had been sold and its great windows dismantled. Then, in a twist of history, Sir Brooke Boothby, a passing Englishman, bought the glass for £200 (about £10,000 in today's money), carried it across the Channel, and sold it at cost-price to his Diocesan Cathedral.

So, almost by accident, possibly the greatest 16th century window glass came to Lichfield – and filled the Cathedral again with colour.

This late-medieval Flemish masterpiece had an enormous influence on English glass studios of the 19th century, many of which rose to the challenge and produced their best work for Lichfield's largest windows.

Two centuries of Black Country industry have now covered the Flemish glass with honest grime, but a multi-million pound programme of conservation will ensure that the seven great windows of Herkenrode should be thoroughly restored by 2015.

A detail from the
Herkenrode windows
in the Lady Chapel

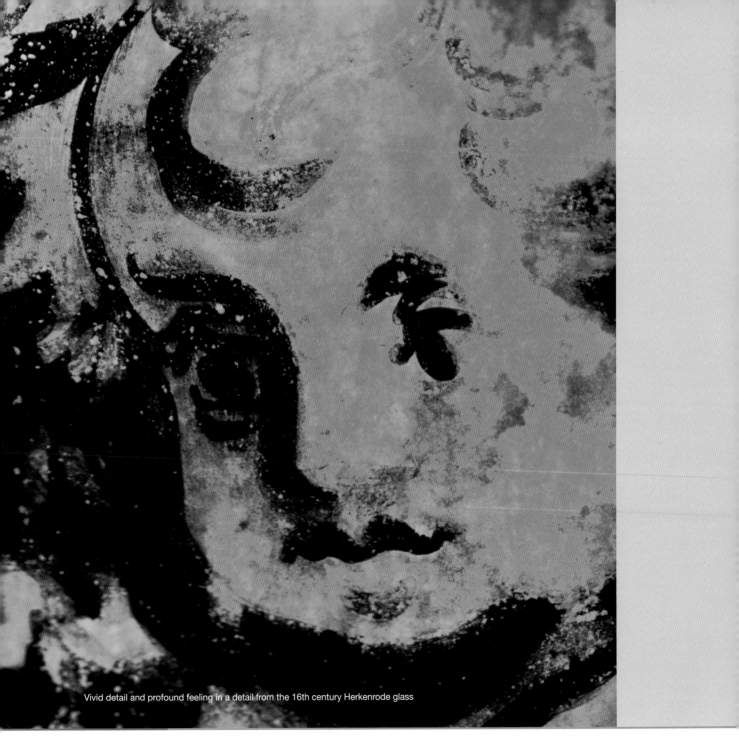

Vivid detail and profound feeling in a detail from the 16th century Herkenrode glass

Besides the Herkenrode glass, the Cathedral has fine examples by Kempe and by Clayton & Bell

RELICS ✚ TREASURES

For 800 years until Henry VIII, the bones of St Chad were honoured inside the Cathedral in a series of ornate shrines. The first, in the 8th century, was a 'little house with a gabled roof and windows'; the last, crafted in the late 14th century, was a silver, gold and jewel-encrusted monument which cost £2,000 (over £1 million in today's money).

Almost from the start, the shrines probably featured an illustrated manuscript of the Gospels and a limestone carving of Mary and Gabriel. At some point, however, the carving was broken and carefully buried; at another, half the manuscript was lost or stolen; then, during the 16th century Reformation, the shrine itself was destroyed and St Chad's bones dispersed.

Half the manuscript, however, has remained in Lichfield for 1000 years. A little younger than the Lindisfarne Gospels and a few years older than the Book of Kells, the priceless 'St Chad Gospels' is one of Europe's most significant books.

Meanwhile, the broken carving lay hidden for centuries – until, during excavation work in 2003, three pieces forming the 'Lichfield Angel' were found in amazing condition under the Cathedral floor.

The beauty of these 8th century relics is repeated all around. Uncovered medieval wall paintings in the Chapter House and Choir Aisle, late-medieval manuscripts in the Library, 16th and 20th century silver in the Sacristy, 19th century metalwork in the Quire – all these, and more, still offer visitors a glimpse of the glories of heaven.

Easily overlooked above a *piscina* in the South Choir Aisle is one of the Cathedral's three medieval wall-paintings

An exquisite detail from a depiction of the Trinity in the South Choir Aisle

The white, pink and lilac palette suggests the Chad Gospels and Lichfield Angel share a common origin

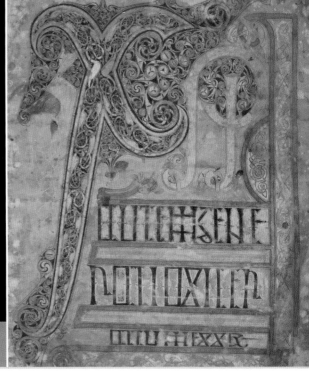

Clockwise from above | The Lichfield Angel; a medieval painting of the Assumption of the Virgin Mary; the Chad Gospels all adorn the Chapter House

STATUES ✠ CARVINGS

If the spires and arches imply that Lichfield's builders were characterised by a certain holy extravagance, the sheer number of their statues and carvings suggests they were gripped by a godly passion for people.

Inside, they carved over seven hundred heads, ranging from tiny two centimetre angels in the Lady Chapel to ranks of half-size humans in the Aisles. If you look up in other Cathedrals you can count the roof-bosses. If you look around in Lichfield, you can lose count of the eyes looking back at you.

It was outside, however, where the masons really set to work. They carved over one hundred life-size statues on the West Front alone: Chad, Saxon kings, famous saints, biblical prophets, Christ and the apostles – today, there's even an incongruous Victoria carved by her daughter Louise.

It must be possible to number the carved heads outside, but nobody has managed it yet. They are not only visible on the walls, but also hidden on the spires, beneath buttresses, tucked into valleys. A few are inside the roof and never see daylight.

If the medieval masons did, in part, build their Cathedral as a very English symbol of God's kingdom, their carvings suggest it's filled with ordinary people who've gone ahead – and are now looking down urging visitors on in joyful anticipation.

There is an astonishing array of carved heads in the Cathedral, not least in the North Choir Aisle

A selection of carvings in wood and stone, inside and outside the Cathedral, from the 12th–19th centuries

MUSIC ✠ WORSHIP

For 1300 years, Cathedral life has centred on offering God the praise he is due. Unlike most medieval cathedrals, Lichfield was never home to a community of monks offering a constant cycle of worship. Here, instead, resident clergy, local laity, skilled musicians and visiting pilgrims have always shared the work.

In 822, Bishop Aethelwald appointed a provost and nineteen canons as the focus of spiritual life. In the 1140s, Bishop de Clinton reorganised the Cathedral and appointed a dean and prebendaries – for whom he provided endowments. With a diocese which spread from Chester to Coventry and Wales to Derby, most prebendaries lived far from the Cathedral – so they paid local 'lay vicars' to sing the services on their behalf.

This pattern still continues – with an addition. During the 16th century, a house was built for the young boys of the Choir, and they've shared in daily worship since.

The praise of God has been silenced only once, for the 14 years following 1646 – when the Cathedral suffered more than almost any other in the Civil War. The central spire was shot down, every roof holed, the bells broken, treasures stolen, statues smashed, carvings de-faced and walls wrecked.

By the Restoration of the Monarchy in 1660, only one resident clergyman, Canon Higgins, and one lay vicar, Zechariah Turnpenny, had survived. They resumed services in the Chapter House – and the daily round of praise and prayer has now been unbroken for almost 350 years.

There has been a Choral Foundation
at Lichfield since at least 1315,
and the praises of God are sung
here daily

The Cathedral supports thriving
regular congregations at Sunday
and midweek services

The combination of pipe organ and human voice remains the staple of English Cathedral Choral tradition in Lichfield as elsewhere. The Cathedral Choir of men and boys is supplemented by the Cathedral Chamber Choir, and by the Cathedral School Girls' Choir and Lichfield Cathedral Young Voices

The Bishop of Lichfield
frequently leads the worship
in the Cathedral on major
festival occasions

SCULPTORS ✠ CRAFTSMEN

The ruin of 1660 was rebuilt in nine years, due to the energy of Bishop Hacket, the memory of Canon Higgins, and the generosity of Charles II – a weather-beaten royal sculpture still stands gratefully by the South Entrance. Together, they restored the gothic masterpiece instead of replacing it with something new and rather Wren-like.

Their work, however, then endured 100 years of neglect and indifference. The city of Lichfield prospered in the 18th century, but its Cathedral experienced decades of decay and decline – until it was virtually unusable again. Finally, in the 1790s, James Wyatt saved it from collapse by removing 500 tons of stone from the Nave vaulting and replacing it with lath and plaster.

All that remains of this period are the Nave ceiling and stone floor – together with the sculptures and memorials of the Lichfield men who flourished in Georgian Britain.

The arrival of glass from Herkenrode, in 1803, launched a recovery. Two works by the greatest sculptor of the age were unveiled in the following decades: Sir Francis Chantrey's masterpiece, 'The Sleeping Children', commemorates the daughters of a cathedral prebendary, and his kneeling image of Bishop Ryder still inspires visitors to pray.

Then, in 1856, a scheme was launched to restore the whole Cathedral – under the direction of Gilbert Scott and his son Oldrid. Completed in 1908, costing a staggering £98,000 (over £30 million in today's money), employing the best local craftsmen, they accomplished the finest Victorian restoration of any British Cathedral. As with the medieval builders before them, their names are nowhere, but their memorial is everywhere.

Sir Francis Chantrey considered 'The Sleeping Children' to be his finest work. He left a piece of uncarved stone under the foot of one of the two girls in the statue, saying 'Only God creates perfection'.

The Skidmore screen illustrates the maxim of the Victorian Cathedral Architect, George Gilbert Scott, who said, 'Let the spirit of the place be the glory of the place'. Here, local materials worked by local craftsmen glorify the God whose gifts they are.

Above I The ornate 19th century Choir Screen by Francis Skidmore and John Birnie Philip **Below I** The marble statue of Bishop Ryder by Sir Francis Chantrey and the bronze bust of Bishop Woods by Sir Jacob Epstein

VAULTING ✠ BOSSES

The restoration of the Chapel of St Chad's Head, in 1897, as a Prayer Chapel, was almost the last piece of Victorian conservation. In medieval times, the skull of St Chad was stored here – and held aloft for pilgrims below to see the precious relic. In the Civil War, however, the Chapel was so severely damaged that it was used only as a store for the next two centuries.

Dean Luckock paid for the restoration himself. He must have had deep pockets, for there is more gilding here than anywhere else in the Cathedral. The golden, carved bosses, depicting incidents from the life of St Chad, are exquisite.

In Lichfield, as in all medieval Cathedrals, the vaulting is studded with carved bosses. Most are regulation florets, which a skilled mason could probably carve blindfolded and left-handed. At the highest points, however, where their work was almost invisible from the floor, they gave free reign to their passions and skill.

The masons would normally have served together in teams, depending on each other for their lives when working on the vaulting and bosses. The central pillar in the Chapter House shows, however, that they did not always achieve complete harmony. The capital seems to have been given to four masons to carve – with each improvising a pattern without any regard to the others.

The beauty of these bosses is easily missed from below. This example is to be found 57 feet above the floor of the Sanctuary

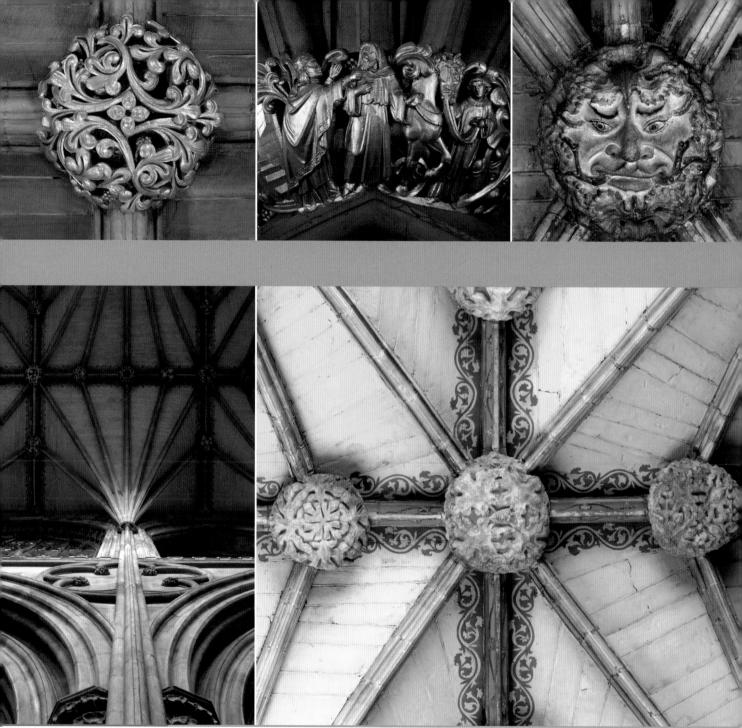

The splendid vaulting above
the Chapter House

FABRIC ✠ STITCHWORK

The work of the medieval builders has been adapted, embellished, restored and refurbished so often during the last 900 years, that every century has left its mark. The building now tells wonderful stories in stone and glass, in tile and metalwork, in sculpture, manuscript and song. It bears witness to the coming and flourishing of the Christian faith in England, but also carries the scars of many pivotal events.

The 12th century, for example, left Norman stones and lawyers' statutes, the 13th gothic curves and carved ceilings, and the 14th wall paintings and rare manuscripts. The 15th century gave perpendicular windows, the 16th stained glass, the 17th sword marks and the 18th an avenue of lime trees. The 19th provided metalwork and floor tiles, the 20th floodlights and fire alarms – and, already, the 21st has presented a mechanical altar platform.

Stone columns, wooden seats, marble statues, wrought ironwork, even vellum manuscripts – all these testaments to (traditionally) male skills have lasted for centuries. Fabric has a much shorter life, so the stitchwork in every century by generations of (traditionally) female embroiderers has faded, withered and been lost for ever.

For over 1000 years, vestments, altar cloths and banners have added a visual dimension to Cathedral worship. Today, the oldest functioning piece of embroidered fabric dates from only the 19th century – so, every Tuesday afternoon, Lichfield Broderers still gather to sew for the glory of God.

The cushions in the aisles celebrate the 431 parishes across the Diocese served by the Mother Church. The flags in the South Transept commemorate the many battles fought by the Staffordshire Regiment. And every hand-sewn altar cloth and clergy vestment reflects a particular spiritual season and summons visitors to the Cathedral's main work of worship.

Some examples of the different styles of stitchwork used in the Cathedral

GLORIA IN EXCELSIS DEO

PATRONS
✠ PILGRIMS

There are three main statues in Lichfield city centre: Smith, captain of the Titanic; Johnson, compiler of the first dictionary, and Boswell, companion of Johnson. There are also small memorials to Garrick and Darwin, but no sign of Chad.

Chad came from Lindisfarne, in 669, as fifth Bishop of Mercia – the midland realm of Anglo-Saxon England. In under three years at Lichfield, until he died of plague, established the Christian faith across the region.

There's no statue in Lichfield, either, for Bishop de Clinton – who developed the town to cater for pilgrims, nor for Bishop de Langton who brought wealth to the city – after installing a dazzling shrine as a pilgrim attraction.

Inside the Cathedral, naturally, there are many memorials to dead clerics, from Dean Heywode's gruesome 15th century tomb to the beautiful 19th century memorial to Bishop Selwyn – possibly Lichfield's greatest bishop since Chad.

What's also missing, of course, in both city and cathedral, is a monument to the millions of ordinary visitors and pilgrims who've been drawn through the centuries to Lichfield. Hundreds of thousands still come each year to the Cathedral: they might now arrive by car rather than by cart, but their reasons for coming are not very different from their predecessors.

Some come to gaze at an architectural wonder; others to be moved by music and treasures. Many come, however, as they have through the ages, to draw close to God in a deeply sacred space. They come, seeking divine inspiration and – inside Lichfield Cathedral – they find their Heart's Desire.

Minton ceramic tiles from the memorial to Bishop Selwyn in the Lady Chapel

Above | A 19th century Minton ceramic tile which honours the 12th century Bishop De Clinton
Below | The Cathedral viewed from across Stowe Pool

Above | A 19th century statue of St. Chad **Below |** A procession leaving the medieval Vestibule and the Victorian font in the North Transept

AROUND ✠ ABOUT

When someone climbs the stone stairs and stands in the central spire, it's hard to imagine how such a structure was built almost 800 years ago – with hand tools and wooden ladders. The builders' skill is plain, but the panorama demands attention – for the masons created the best vantage point in the Midlands.

Peering down between the spires, past the expanse of roofs, there's the circuit of Britain's most complete Cathedral Close – including Darwin House and Vicars' Close. Beyond are the remains of the 12th century moat; and east across Stowe Pool, the well where Chad baptised converts.

Few Cathedrals dominate the city skyline more than Lichfield. The town lies south, over the Minster Pool across which pilgrims had to row, past the Market Square with St. Mary's Heritage Centre and the Johnson Birthplace Museum.

Instead of rowing, today's visitors cross a dam on foot, but – like their medieval counterparts – they're drawn by the breath-taking spires that are still raising three cheers to God.

At the start of the new millennium, a fresh wave of determination to restore and rebuild has arisen – a godly desire to turn Lichfield into the most sustainable, inspirational, well equipped and best interpreted Cathedral in Britain.

The plans are made. The work has begun. There's a new shrine to create and old treasures to conserve. There are buttresses to restore, toilets to install, equipment to replace and a beautiful centre to build for the pilgrims of tomorrow.

Millions need raising (about £13 million – in today's money!). But the line of Hedda, de Clinton, de Langton, Hacket, Wyatt and Scott has not been exhausted. The Cathedral with an extraordinary past has an even more glorious future. Lichfield Inspires.

The view east from inside the
central spire, looking over Stowe
Water towards Derbyshire

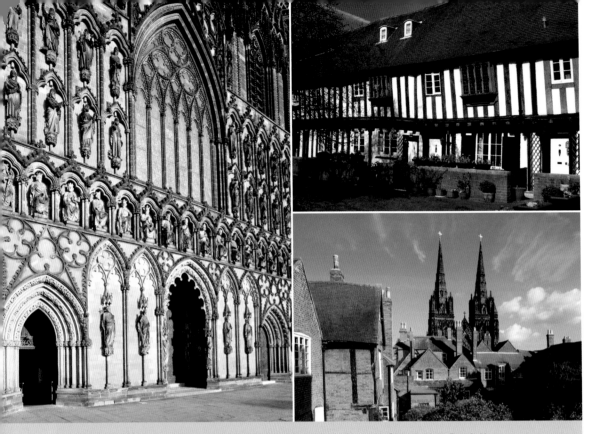

Clockwise from above I The elaborately decorated West Front; Vicars' Close; the Cathedral from Darwin House
Below I Dam Street and the City from the central spire.

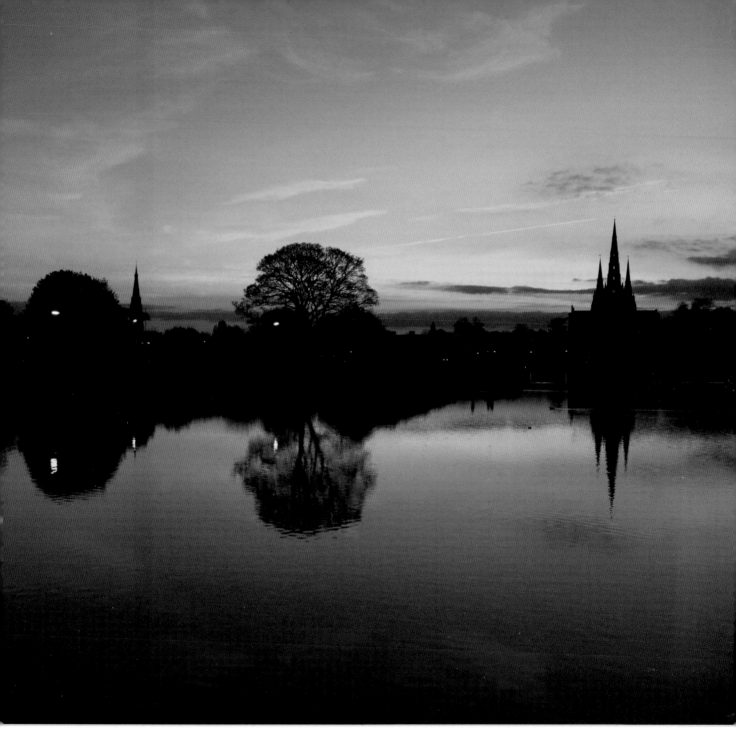

'Jesus Christ is the same, yesterday, today and forever'

Hebrews 13.8